ON MY WAY HERE

On My Way Here

Paul Bukovec

CONTENTS

1

INTRO: GRATEFUL

For the resilience antibody
I carry in my Eastern European
blood, genetic inheritance
from my father's side
for defense against
the immigrant inferiority
complex he left me in the will.

For grandma's broken English;
for dad's barely balanced chip.
For mom's long suffering
devotion to raising us as special
to soothe her from her loss.

For an impossibly pious
seminarian uncle who shone
a path from which
to later turn.

For parents from brief
schooling who scuffled

through a great depression
and gale force moods
through sheer determination
and work that proved that
they were really something
more than what they felt.

For my people who learned
their social graces awkwardly,
who spurned ten dollar words,
who cooked food reverentially,
and ate it like communion.

For playing in the street
with hordes of second generation
kids who mocked each other's
nationalities while being lured
by smells from strange apartment
windows to taste food in neighbor's
kitchens, to disappoint
their own people by loving girls
and boys not their kind.

For catholic school, in spite
of all its cruelties, for
drilling me and other peasant children
in skills both rote and analytical.
For the private-prep-school
on-the–cheap beyond wild
dreams or means. For finding
there a voice and diction
and encouragement to ask.

For Candy Palangelo, the fast
and busty cheerleader from the public
high across the street who touched my thigh
in the Mayfair Theater balcony and
drove me scurrying back to books.

For wandering unaware and
unready into 1963 New York.
For stumbling headlong
into college just when so much
was jumping off:

For the history-of-ideas curriculum
I did not know to expect; for the Tourette's
beeping reference librarian who
showed me where to find the gems.

For the Village Vanguard, Gerde's
Folk City, the Lower East Side,
the Thalia, the drama club,
concerts in the park, anti-war
marches, draft counseling, weed,
Denise Levertov at St Marks,
the Berrigans in Harlem.

For the sister school sweeties
I finally felt ready for
before they thought they were.
For the start of a lifelong practice
of long walks to calm my crazies.

For the dumbest random luck
imaginable to happen along

when I could hump a union
factory summer job to pay
the fare for an outrageous
education in the baddest city
at the very craziest of moments
to become a bleeding hearted
liberal/commie/artsy/conscientious
objector emerging without debt except
for what I still owe in love and gratitude
to family, friends, and the exquisite
accidents from where and when and
how I came such a distance.

2

ORIGIN STORIES: CONCRETE WONDER PARK

Came up in north jersey in the fifties:
bounced the streets to proto-techno
embroidery factory machine beats.
had sidewalk wrestling matches
on cardboard shipping boxes,
played stick ball, ring-a-levio,
cowboys and indians, war games
with spools and tubes... (ammo
gathered from factory trash), tackle
football in the park, snow ball fights
(with igloo forts and arsenals)
endless sledding, bike riding
in small posses, tar beach,

the umbrella man, the shoemaker's,
the candy store, corner pizza, the avenue,
the live chicken butcher store, forties cars

with running boards, sticks that morphed
into swords and guns. the man-hunt game
we called Rabies, weenie roasts down the cliffs...

we had doting moms; moody, working
class dads with green-horn legacies,
and scuffling lessons from the great
depression. most of our parents did
not finish high school. we ran mostly
with other second-generation kids from
european immigrants: mixing, mocking,
loving, fighting and teasing each other
all round the neighborhood. public
school kids and catholic school kids.
irish, itallian, slav, german, and polish.

staged our pirate raids, duels. sieges,
stage coach robberies, and shipwrecks.
had countless stick ball games,
two-hand-touch contests, foot races.

our arcade was in the corner
luncheonette, where you put your nickel
up on the pinball glass, called "next"
and held the machine as long as luck or
pocket change allowed. on flush occasions,
we'd have an egg-cream, a soda-fountain
float or penny candy, and schemed up
outings to Palisades Amusement Park
to ride the roller coaster, the mighty mouse,
and swim the largest outdoor salt water
wave pool in the entire universe.

we watched the older boys from afar.
steered clear but stayed curious about
how they lounged, duck-tailed and tee-
shirt sleeves rolled, smoking, cool and
tough, occasionally preparing to do battle
or rumble on some other turf for unknown
causes, affecting Dean and Brando;
their scene evoking more concrete jungles
than wonder parks, maybe because they
reimagined movies very different than
our own, having come up harder and
faster, before the second war had ended,
and television had begun. jersey man/boys
fronting tough guys like Marlon on the waterfront
who coulda/shoulda been a contender...

3

GUS, TESSIE, AND CHUBBY

Gus and Tessie lived
next door on our landing.
top floor; fourth floor
walk up. kept three
spaniels in their bathroom
you could smell under
the door. and hear too
whenever they sensed
anybody breaking for
the stairs to a freedom they
could faintly recall.

Gus wore a watch cap.
and a grey-white tee.
old jeans jacket.
dungarees,
wide roll cuffs.
three days shadow
on his face.

butt hanging
from his lip.
blotchy tattoos,
both forearms.
scuffed work boots.

yellow saw teeth
peeped out
on that rare
occasion of
a Gus smile.
then his eyes
would twinkle
ever so.

Tessie was a thick squat
woman of indiscernible age.
genially slovenly.
hair combed
with her fingers.
mostly wore stained
black slacks
or a spotty skirt.
dark blouse:
two pounds of beans
in a pound and a half sack.
chain smoked camels.
hacked like tuberculosis.
cursed like a sailor.
frequently knocked
on our door hawking stuff
that "fell off a truck."
mom would decline.

Gus and Tessie called
their son Chubby,
which he wasn't.
might have been in his
twenties. parked his chopper
on the sidewalk. duck tail.
black leather jacket.
brought random
girls home in the afternoon
to the empty flat. could hear
thumping through the wall
of my bedroom. I thought
they were wrestling.
I was only eight.

Gus and Tessie worked
embroidery factories nearby.
also worked a few hustles.
numbers, hot goods,
cigarettes from down south.
never knew for sure what,
other than ride cycle,
Chubby did with his time. ride,
and thump in the afternoons.

one day climbing stairs
coming from school I passed
Chubby and that afternoon's
delight descending
flushed and tousled
from above.
she looked away.

he seemed unusually
sheepish. nodded.
more like bowed his
head. embarrassed.
it was 1954. this rebel
had no cause to be
ashamed facing me,
a little twerp heading home
from catholic school.
but it seemed like
he was.

sometime later
when I realized what
those strange noises
emanating from
next door
we're all about,
it all made sense.

Tessie, Gus,
and Chubby
we're long gone
by then. scuttled
off suddenly
one night
leaving only
the odor of cockers
and dust bunnies
in their wake.

my folks whispered
in the kitchen

about the law
and "shenanigans".
heard the word
"shady" a lot.
Also, a Croatian word
that meant "shabby".

they were rarely,
if ever,
mentioned
after that.

4

AUTUMN SCENES: A BOYS'S LIFE IN NORTH JERSEY

age seven

the boy is feverish. bundled on the
couch against the tenement chill. his mom,
washer woman in babushka and house
coat, hauls loads from the kitchen

to the living room window, pins laundry
on the line, sends it out across the breach.
bustles back to the kitchen. dutiful. methodical.
dumping baskets. sorting piles. pulling garments

from the swirling drink, she twists and feeds
them to the wringer. fidgets dials.
marches a new batch to the alley gallows.
mom yanks her kerchief back mid-trip, sweat

beading on her upper lip. fishes out another

catch; wrestles it between the rollers, but
ensnares the loose end of her headscarf in her rush.
all at once, she's wrenched and flailing.

a choke hold struggle: cheek and jowl against
the rubber maw. the boy, helpless.
the mom, red faced. gasping.
after far too long, she slaps a desperate hand
against the panel and the death grip is released.

mom spins quickly round to find her boy
a stunned survivor-witness. in the joyous
head-on clutch, hot faces collide. tears
smear hard against each other's cheeks.

age eight

crisp afternoon. college football on the set. I am
rooting for the guys in black but more intent on
soldiers gathered on the rug, ambushed now by
commandos rushing from behind a pillow mountain.

earlier today my dad climbed the clothes line pole
four stories up to change the rope. high near the top,
he rode the sway: pirate on the main mast.
neighbor kids applauded. dad looked unfazed.

circus act complete, standing at the living room
window, he fishes line up from the alley, then sits
backwards on the sill: body out, legs inside,
and reaches up to thread the pulley.

the black team scores. GIs surge across

the carpet. A scuffling distracts over in the corner.
I glance up just in time to see dad's torso vanish.
only legs remain, splayed wide against each jamb,
toes praying to the ceiling.

after an eternal pause, one hand haltingly
emerges from beneath, grabs hold the frame,
and slowly pulls himself up into the room,
red faced, wobbly upright, head shaking.
he sighs. looks embarrassed but relieved.

stares right by me. *don't tell your mother!*
walks on past, through the kitchen, out
the apartment door, and down the hallway stairs.
honored to be so trusted, I am tight-lipped.
put my soldiers in the drawer; shut off the TV,
and stare out the window at the concrete below.

age nine

first foray into
mischief night:
raggedy clothes.
pockets stuffed with chalk.
socks filled with flour. knotted
watch cap for a helmet.
our boy tramps down
eight flights
to join the melee:.
street fighting man.

white slashes.
powder billowing

with every blow
connected.
swinging wildly.
dueling.
taking on
all comers.

epic donnybrook.
cast of thousands:
Zorro. Musketeers.
The Count of Monte Cristo.
Crocket at the Alamo.
wide screen
epic battle scenes.

till, in a jolt, the action breaks.

coated in flour dust
and chalk,
arm weary,
bloodlust waning.
the warriors
stand
panting

Eugene yells:
"let's go do
Mr. Dokker's windows:
that bastard has it coming !!! "

vigilantes now,
kids race
screaming.

our boy, caught up,
frenzied,
joins in.

a gooey mass:
raw eggs,
chewed up tootsie roll
curb dirt
thrown up on the glass.

all at once our boy is squeamish.

the angry rush,
too much.
the contagion,
scary.
this revenge,
too harsh, too mean.

mom's disappointed frown hovers over him.

sure, the old man is a grouch.
always ranting about noise,
trash, sneakers on the wires.
always on stealth
patrol in front
of his ground floor flat
hassling the bejesus out of kids.

yet and still, our boy
feels an urge
to stand up.
call out

to the guys to stop
the rampage.

can't muster a voice.
can't find the courage
to go against the crowd.

can only slink away,
muted by fear.
ashamed.

next day the evidence
gleamed bright
in the morning sun
both panes
varnished
in a veneer
like frozen vomit.

Dokker was rarely
seen thereafter.

left the mess up
through the winter.
moved the following spring.

past the house
each day on his way to school
our boy turned his head.
blinked rueful
at the memory
of that fateful night
when he might have

been man enough
to fill his costume.
but wasn't.

5

THINGS I LEARNED FROM MY MOM

The feeling of being cherished.
The joy and reverence for home cooking.
A predisposition to excessive worry.
Eastern European hospitality.
Distrust of the rich.
The love of a bargain.
Recreational shopping.
Germ vigilance.
An eye for fashion.
To "do my best".
Sensitivity for the underdog.
To pursue my interests.
Nesting.
An appreciation of gossip.
To expect disappointment in relationships.
An enthusiasm for hard work.
The value of a hug.
Disgust with pomposity.
A mistrust of joy.

To always cook more than is needed.
The comfort of women.
Respect for elders while recognizing their faults.
Unease in restaurants.
To guard my boundaries.
Sensitivity to criticism.
The satisfaction of a well told story.
A knee jerk reaction to unsolicited advice.
A predilection for ample breasts.

6

NEAR THE END

Mom's dementia
ascended slowly
from sticky recesses.

lost her skill
with numbers first;
then her sharpness
for games.
Eventually
the darkening
smothered
what small comfort
old photo albums
brought her.

Occasionally
the contacts
seemed to flush
themselves
for brief moments
of clarity

and bright eyes beaming.
But near the end
she looked mostly
through foggy windows.

And she was also scared a lot.

Birds appeared looming
or swooping down
suddenly.
Children on cereal box labels
talked soothingly
to her but noisy neighbors
clattered on the roof.

Phantasms turned
knobs in the night.

But up until near the very
end, she loved a visit.

Could turn a light on in the
dim recesses and glow gratefully
whilst confabulating
a gathering of her
imagined bearings.

Once, around this time,
I went to her room
to help her to lunch
from her recliner
catty-cornered
next to the mirrored

sliding door closet,
opposite the TV.

Bending forward
to rise out of her chair,
she caught the gaze of
a rumpled old grey woman
smiling back
at her from the glass.
Proudly proclaimed
to the lady in the
reflection:
"This is my son"

"How do you do?" I said.

"She's a very nice woman"
mom stage whispered
confidentially
tilting her head
toward the closet door.

"I'm sure she is." I said,
as matter of fact as possible.

Then we trundled off to eat our lunch.

Weeks later she fell
from bed into delirium
and sepsis and a shocked
silence she broke
only to pray and call out
in Croatian.

I like to think grandma
Anna then appeared to
join the feverish
rosary recitations
begging the other mother,
Mary, to *pray for us sinners*

And that in the end
they were all very nice women.
together with each other.

7

HOBOKEN SCION

She hallucinates
Bosnian women making
Turkish coffee
at the nursing station,
memories bleeding through,
pentimento.

Asks me outright,
no need to beat around the bush:
You look familiar, who are you?
I'm Paul, Grandma, Rudy's son.
Paulie? Little Paulie? All grown up?
You were always such a nice boy.
But that Rudy! Majka majija!
WHAT A PAIN IN MY HEART!!

Grandma Sophie
married young
to an older
Croat baker.
Had six kids.

Four survived.
Three darling spit curls.
One cowlick.
Rudy always went
the other way.
Stubborn.
Picky eater.
Antsy all the time.
Ran the Hoboken streets
with the Italians.
Rode his bike
like a child possessed,
crashed his motor cycle
outside a police station.
Jumped the ferry turnstiles
to New York
with Frankie Sinatra.
Combed his hair
like Valentino.

His father lit one cigarette
off the last.
Overworked
his immigrant heart
till it exploded in his chest,
mid-forties.
The Great Depression ate
the family bakery
like a pecan Danish.
Rudy went to work
straight out of grade school.
Hated the German shops.

The Jews used the best in-gree-da-ments,

so he rode the bus
into Manhattan.
Hardest working man
in every kitchen.
Took no shit.
Would walk right out
and find another job.
Nobody's donkey!

Found a used Yoga book
in a bin and taught
himself to be a pretzel.
Stood on his head
in the middle
of the living room:
upside down lotus.
Neighborhood kids
thought he looked
like Cheyenne Body.
But they were short
and dad was all
of five foot seven:
broad of chest
and swagger.

Moody guy.
Storms blew through suddenly.
Sometimes lightning came
amidst the thunder.
We learned to take cover.
He survived on little sleep,

dark clouds overhead,
cold wind in his face.
We survived
tip toeing round him.
Ranted about processed food,
the government and doctors.
Droned tediously on
about healthy stuff
like vinegar and garlic.
Outlived his few friends.
Too late came to cherish his
wife who died with Alzheimer's
he called crazy.

When it was sundown
at the nursing home
and he was wild eyed rambling,
he let me in on his best kept secret:
His mother never really liked him much
and his dad didn't hardly either.

8

MY FATHER'S HANDS

my father had
incredibly strong hands
that began working
in the family bakery
at a very early age
and rarely stopped
thereafter.

those hands kneaded
tons of bread and cake
dough; made a million rolls
and pastries and
cookies and cakes;
chipped and caulked
the hulls of war ships
in the Hoboken shipyard;
built truck bodies
for Adam Black;
worked on family cars
at all hours;
dug gardens,

trimmed shrubberies,
shoveled snow,
and mended, and patched,
and cleaned
a myriad of things.

they were experienced hands:
big wide palms and
broad thick fingers.

usually there was
a recent cut or gouge
whose healing was delayed
by the constant motion.
permanently
calloused,
weathered,
surprisingly deft,
my father's hands
could always handle
seriously hot objects.

proud working-class hands.
not catching or throwing hands.
not especially playful hands.
not caressing or soothing hands.

they could occasionally
be angry, violent hands.

hands that struck
suddenly and hard:
awe-fully strong hands

that felt like padded clubs
against the head or shoulders.

hard love hands
that were also
generous hands
willing to help
family or strangers
or give the shirt off his back
or slip a twenty
or wrap up some goodies
to take away from a visit

and artistic hands
creating bouquets of flowers
atop luscious cakes
with beautiful scrolled script
with delicate loops and
filigree flourishes.
hands that mixed colors
of icings and fillings
with minced nuts and fruit jams
and french creams
and drizzled chocolates.

hands that
whipped potatoes
so fluffy and thick
they seemed imagined.

they were strong hands
attached to strong arms
that also bore many scars

of oven burns
and nicks and cuts
from reaching
in and under
and around
so many projects.

and his shoulders
were broad.
And his ribcage
formed the slats
of a moderately sized
barrel chest.

but he was,
surprisingly,
not a big man.
he was, in fact,
a welter-weight
who came on
like a light-heavy.

my father was also
a hand cruncher:
one of those men
who insist on making
a rather painfully
strong impression
while shaking hands
with other men.

earlier in his life,
perhaps it was

to make it clear
that he was
way stronger
than he looked.
he was.

later in his life,
perhaps it was to show
that he was still
very powerful.
he was.

nowadays
he isn't
as much.

his eyes fail him
his legs are constantly aching
his stamina is waning
his ninety-odd
year old hands
have begun to lose
the firmness
of their grip

and his fingers.
have started to lose
the feeling
at their ends

they can no longer
easily master
the many tasks

he still attempts:
keeping busy
to chase away
the harpies
of remorse, regret
and loneliness

when I visit
he's always doing
some chore:
repainting
re-cleaning
rearranging
digging and chopping
washing and cooking
and baking and baking

he looks small and wiry.
wild and teary eyed
mid motion
semi startled
tatty and disheveled
in worn out work clothes
that are clean
but un-mended

he rarely stops
what he is doing
and often takes
a while, if at all
to change gears
and address
his visitor

and when he does
there are long
reminiscences
about work
or diatribes
about the systems
or lecturettes
about healthy eating.

and somewhere
in the midst of
all this, I move
gingerly closer to him
and he lets me
button his shirt
passively
like a small boy
shaking his head
a bit ruefully.

and I look
down at those
remarkable hands
amidst my own
remorse and regret
and with a sad
wistful nostalgia
for this closeness
rarely felt
with my father's hands.

9

2. JOURNEYS

Passing on the road in Africa, 1970

The sun-baked road shimmers past
evaporating mirage puddles
to the North Roundabout
before veering sharply into Lusaka.
At the mile marker
a besotted old pick-up careens
past close enough to almost smell
the drunk driver rushing too wildly up
to the keepy-lefty to stop before the merge.
He skids sideways into the traffic circle
on two wheels, flips into a side roll,
tumbles all the way over,
and lands, right side up again.

The sub-Saharan glare allows no shadows.

A nappy black head dangles out
the driver's side window, dark rivulets stream
down the dull white door.

Pedestrians rush up:
mothers with kitenge strapped babies,
old men on ancient bikes,
women balancing plastic water pails,
adolescents with hands to shocked faces.
I stop. Sit stunned and unsure.
Then walk boldly through the parting crowd.
I surprise myself by opening the truck door
to catch the frail dead weight falling
into my arms. Lay him on the tarmac,
feel for his heart; turn his head
to let the blood out.
He is gone.

And I am Bwana without portfolio.
Lone European, officiously fearless.
Self-appointed "in-charge",

as clueless as anyone
about what to do next.
Unabashedly out
in front of it all:
Head bowed, red faced,
I wait till the police arrive.

Then slip away.

10

NORMA

met Norma on a commuter bus
between Jersey and the City.
late thirties, business-casual.
auburn rinsed perm. light make-up.
faint, nervous smile. friendly eyes
glancing towards the empty seat.

I was damaged goods, broken
hearted at the time. twenty-five.
scruffy. tousled, wild haired.
just back from several years
teaching overseas. shipwrecked
by a turbulent breakup.
washed ashore, still adrift.
restless. beset. stung.

plopped down beside her.
emboldened by the hint
of possible permission. smiled.
her face opened. welcomed.
we exhaled together. spoke.

turned out Norma had her own
sad story which she blurted
bluntly to me shortly after
greetings and other niceties,
assuming, most likely, she'd
never see my face again.

surprised each other: exchanged
numbers in the Port Authority Bus
Terminal. met later that evening.
she had dressed down. I had
spruced a bit. still mismatched
odd-fellows. each hungry; each
leaning precariously. at risk
of falling. both finding comfort
in the kind familiar strangeness
of the other. shared a meal. went
to her place for dessert.

Norma's husband had recently
departed to pursue other fellas,
leaving within her a confidence
crisis half the size of manhattan.
mostly to compensate, and
possibly, also, to augment
her income as a psychiatric social
worker, Norma had found part time
employment in a massage parlor
on the east side, across from
Alexander's Department Store.

there she and her very generous

breasts got lots of positive regard,
there Gay Talese worked
the reception desk researching
his next best seller, and there
told Norma regularly that
a nice, middle-class jewish girl
like she really didn't belong.

spent the summer together
agreeing that it would not,
could not be for keeps.
different generations.
opposite sides of the boomer
divide. too wide a gap
to stand astride. too much
counter culture, music, politics
in the way. but for two sweet
months we engaged in lovely
semi-foreign exchange.

browsed shops. noshed
exotic cuisines. walked Cental
Park. cruised the Village.
shopped Zabar's. frequented
the Thalia. the Waverly.

she introduced me to the opera,
to Tanglewood string quartets.
I introduced her to jazz,
the Village Vanguard. my
acid rock, a bridge too far. but
she loved my home cooked meals,
my enthusiastic, grateful loving.

she, herself, was thankful:
deep-sigh-relieved to be so
rigorously desired. so often.
such a change. affirmation.

helped her move to a smaller
flat. mourn her dog lost
to divorce. got her off to work
on mornings when she least
felt like going... struggling to
be there for others while just
coming home to her own self.

soothed, encouraged one
another best we could. she urged
my search for training; new career
goals. abandoned her east
side parlor gig by mid-July.
by August I was accepted
to a program in Philly.

braced ourselves. quarreled
briefly. ignored inevitabilities
a few more weeks. tried to gently
tug apart the tangled roots
recently but firmly entwined.

there was some tearing, despite
our cautious, careful planning.
gratitudes overwhelmed by
anticipated losses. old wounds
throbbing in new places.

finally we resolved to part
warmly. resigned to the inevitability
of our original understanding.
exchanging hugs and pangs.
tearful wishes for best possible
lives. no plans to keep in touch.
neither wanting fresh scabs to rip.

accidental lovers. hitch hikers
who picked each other up along the road.
going separate ways, appreciative
to have shared the same leg of different
journeys, but not our final destinations.

11

FORCED MARCH 2001

got driven to new york city
on a chilly wet sunday morning
by a gnawing need to take in
the horror and the holy aftermath
of the jihad guided missiles.

parked in the twenties on the eastside
and walked down past hundreds of faces
desperately pasted on walls and fences
and fixed atop bodies
moving to a quiet funereal beat
pounding a solemn silent march
inside so many minds
distracted and distraught
while candles still flickered
in the drizzle
and urgent messages
began to run in inky rivulets
down pages posted to find
but left finally

to honor the forever lost.

wandered through Union Square,
now fairly desolate
without the impromptu staging sites
for improvised memorials and silent vigils
a sadly empty rain slicked
grimly grimy place of passage
to the lower depths of manhattan,
the "clean up" leaving dirt embedded puddles
of melted wax and scraps of paper
stuck to where tape still clung
to fences and pavements...

and the air changed quickly crossing 14th street.
Picked up wisps of smoke as I quickened my pace,
and walked headlong down past
villagers and college students on broadway through
almost normal new york bustle wondering
how and where and if these people carry on
or if the guy spinning his kid on the Cooper Union Cube
could smell the same smoke I was smelling
or if all the empty chic clothing stores round NYU
were in mourning this morning
for the death of stylish decadence
or outrageous and conspicuous consumption
for which the corpse like mannequins
beckoned vapidly from post-modern shop windows
as I bore down and the rain fell even harder.

and crossing Houston, the air changed utterly

the soho/suburban/boho passersby

suddenly and surreptitiously seemed
enveloped by the increasingly acrid
powdery stench that thickened the atmosphere
constricting and coating passageways and
tightening eyes and lips and drawing faces into taut
sad seriousness ever more gravely the further I marched
to the end of the island

and the streets became clogged with
new york style humanity and lots
of flag pins and scarves and souvenir pictures
and reverentially serious Koreans
selling symbols and mementos
and stern-faced cops and wooden sawhorses
and cameras and dust masks and
painfully solemn faces and
softly speaking or mostly mute adults
craning necks and standing on tippy toes
and bunching up and looking back
like Lot's wife petrified in guilty
morbid fascination while the
cops called out to keep on moving
through the ashen streets and
the choking dust and I walked on
as the skyscraping mausoleums
ringing the disaster
mouthlessly moaned and
stared down with empty dirty eyes
and people took color digital movies
of a black and white surreal landscape
where all motion seemed frozen and
the steady rain could not wash
away the smell of cremated concrete

and asbestos and bodies and plastic and
plaster and paper and electronics and metal and
innocence and arrogance and big and small business
and life as we knew it.

and I turned a corner to dodge the crowd
and turned once more onto a dreamscaped side
street coated in desert moon dust with an old woman
disguised as an epiphany freeze framed in the middle
of the narrow road bent over a tripod with a parenthesis
for a back shooting her own epiphanous moment:

framed in a doorway bordered on top by a sign that read
NEW YORK STOCK EXCHANGE stood an ash covered
military man still as a Buckingham Guard in a blizzard,
dust mask on his face and a statue's resolve.

I finally stood still, watching the motionless old
photographer framing the immovable sentinel
at the gate of the world's trading temple which
was not destroyed in the fall of the towers, but
now looked like it stood on a street in Kabul,
Afghanistan. And I saw why they came.

and how bitter it tasted...

12

ABRUPTED ON ELECTRIC AVENUE

I was 56 and pure white of hair but mercifully immature enough to have refused to grow out of a never-ending fascination with certain ongoing shifts along the boundaries of music and cultural trends where the edgy and marginal meet the popular and trendy. And as far back as Catholic School, I always liked to dance.

Jimi may have started it all, but I got my head seriously dislocated from my whip lashed ass by the poly rhythmic fusions of different seventies jazz rockers branching out from Miles and Herbie and Fela and King Sunny; and then I got my spine syncopatedly funked up by George Clinton, Wa Wa Watson and Bernie Worrell.

African drums drew me deep into World Music in the eighties. Juju and Soukous and Zouk and Township Jive and Reggae pushed my pulse, pumped my blood, gave my knees and torso new ways to relate. And then there was Prince and Chaka and even Madonna on the home front and the dance remixes in the bins at Sounds of Market Street where lots of the extended plays flashed through long jazzy grooves, and that incredibly sexy woman on the jacket of Black Box compelled me to buy the vamp and the soulful beseeching wail that would haunt me and lure me deeper into club music.

And then it all got so much more electric and eclectic when the posses formed in London and Bristol and I was grabbed up soul to Soul ll Soul, my body entranced by those grooved hypnotic beats. And somewhere in the nineties, I saw Tricky at the TLA, got sucked into Trip Hop and Acid Jazz and swept along from those dark eddies into the spinning whirlpools of electronica and the choppy turbulence of progressive hip hop.

And surreptitiously House Music became a guilty pleasure I enjoyed secretly away from most of my peers, usually driving both me and my car to and from work or even more deeply on monthly forays to dance clubs with a small band of like-minded peter pans and tinker bells for periodic bustamovathons.

I started, also, to occasionally drift through places like Silk City or the now very dearly departed Revival or the defunct Smoke or Palmer's Social Club alone on my way back from some other event to absorb the beats, work up a solitary shvitz and roll on home. I learned to stay in my own orbit when soloing at these spots since I was, even back then, considerably older than most of the crowd. Basically, it felt like mutual noninvolvement pact. I was there for the bass and drum lines. I kept to myself while taking in the music and the scene and episodically dancing alone in the crowd. Inside my own circle, inside the music. Feelin it.

I've always had lots of Funk and R&B in my music collection, especially for the yearly house parties we've thrown for the last couple of decades. But cookin alone in my kitchen the sound track is now likely to be stuff like Massive Attack, or Groove Armada, or Kruder and Dorfmeister, or Thievery Corporation, or DJ Krush, or Wagon Christ.. More often than not, I just wanna hear a good beat. And be moved in the place where I am.

Like the two Chemical Brothers' concerts at the Electric Factory I caught and was electrocuted by the energy, and sheer excitement and exhilaration of what felt like thousands surging simultaneously to their Svengalian twists of dials and shifts of levers.

This summer, a variety of obligations and a fabulous vacation had diverted me from the kind of live music that I love, so those cravings for good thumping, driving electronica overrode my solemn oath to never darken the portals of the Tweeter Center again, and I transnavigated the Delaware late on a Tuesday afternoon for Moby's answer to Lollapalooza to pay forty bucks for a lawn ticket to maybe witness a long list of performers, some of which I even knew like Busta Rhymes, the Blue Man Group, David Bowie and, of course, the little bald guy. But mostly I made the trip to visit the Playstation 2 Dance Tent to experience the raving light and sound storm of a series of top notch DJ's.

So I set up on the grass, watch and sway to Busta & co, then begin what is to be my wander route for the evening: down across the lawn, past the vending booths, short stop at the water fountains then on into the air blown/cooled tent for an ever darkening evermore light flashing spectacle of twisting jerking fluidly high and bouncing kids frenzied by some very good beats. I move slowly and meanderingly through this maze of revelers stopping briefly to groove a little here and there then I wander out again to return to the lawn for a while before I get the wanderlust again...

I'm on about my third tour through the crowds, steppin light, feeling a mostly nice vibe from those I'm sliding around and through catching only the occasional fish eye from somebody or other who wonders what that gray dude is about or makes me for security or a cop or a friend of their father... but mostly I'm fairly oblivious and grooving on the sights and sounds and pretty astounded at the dancing and the music's incredible energy and how much more alive it feels in this balloon of techno and sweat and swirl than out on the lawn too far away from the Duke to feel Bowie's cool burn... and the music gets revved and pumped deeper and higher and I'm practically skipping through the throng as I reach an opening near an edge of dancers and I just stop going forward in my sharklike swerve and move in place suddenly gripped and wracked byandthrough the beat and I'm dancing a kind of spastic snapping flapping funky unfluid freeform gyrate that feels at first self-consciously unlike all the action around me, then allatonce I'M just unfuckingconscious or caring of any shit other than the abandon of the music entering me and leaving having played my meager instrument and plucked all my marionette strings... and just as intensely and suddenly as that electronic tornado picked me up it drops me down and i stagger away wadshot and sweatweary through the crowd.

But off to the side and a little behind me comes this little female person who grabs my arm and whips around the front of me. She is almost yelling to be heard above the storm of sound and it's coming from a very soft nodding and maybe affirming face. I have to turn my ear to her mouth to get whats coming out... " SO HAPPY...YOU CAn RECOGNIZzee/ ...shoW/ and?/ HONOR (?) OUR MUSIC!!!! IT'S JUST SO NIIIIICE!!! JUST WANNA THANK YOU!!! FOR...*+^>! OUR MUSIC..." I mumble/yell back in a voice that barely leaves my lips before it falls suicidally to the floor never reaching her face saying: "I like to dance... " BUT...I want to scream: "IT'S MY MUSIC TOO!!!" but (all of a sudden, I'm melting like the wicked witch, and...) I shake her earnestly outstretched hand and nod at this ecstatic munchkin and then just stagger on out of the tent through what now feels more like a gauntlet of fisheyes up to the water fountains where it seems the young folk are parting ways to let the senior citizen get his much-needed drink...

and I wander endlessly back to my towel on the now very huge lawn and lie down while David Bowie implores us: LET'S DANCE and I look around to notice how differently the audience out here moves to this music than that in the pulsating gigantic condom over there where the tripped out waif assassinated my bliss and left me limp and lonely and impossibly ancient by thanking me so profusely for being some kind of a music time traveler to, but not actually part of this scene at all: just a groovy old guy showing props to the kids. And here I thought I was some subset of one in that raving mass of integers just grooving differently, separate but equal... Nah.

And, honestly, I know that little gal meant well by me. And that she had no idea how my vulnerable psyche was gonna momentarily collapse in that moment of interruption and bubblebursting recognition of my (remarkable to her) presence. And the truth is I've always known somewhere down deep inside that not only have I probably stood too long at the dance, but back in my thirties when I started following the thumping out into the places where the tribal sounds stirred primal movements and feelings, I was already a bit late to that party. But it has been a wonderful Ride On Time. And Time will tell you, if you bend your ear to listen, that music and movement are great ways to feel timeless and forever young, but the beat does go on. Within you and without you. And eventually it gets easier to tell the dancer from the dance

.

13

GOOD FRIDAY, LIMPING TOWARD REDEMPTION

morning sun
pierces
the canopy
filtering
stained glass light
on the forest floor

leaf mulch rot,
and evergreen musk
incense this chapel

I limp along
a path
shadowed
by memories
of mumbled
prayers
stabat maters
and homilies

for
every
station

my hamstring ache
a minor
mortification
that recalls
long past
fasts and
hard benched
observances
of calvary
and the passion
of a cross
which now
a staccato
woodpecker
suggests
might be
a hollow
rotted
tree
on the trail
away from
penance
pomp
and
the circumstance
of robed men
hiding
in swollen
veiled

hypocrisies.

I cross a gully

spring rain
has washed
through here
leaving
a rush of buds
wild chirpings and
daffy celebrations

the woods
are amok:
beatific
redemptions,
rebirths,
resurrections

my procession
shuffles forward
with thoughts
of May poles,
satyrs, fawns
and dancing girls

I gimp
gleefully
determined
to commemorate
this year's
salvation
with reimagined

ancient rites
and pagan
rituals:

joyous
heathen
tributes
to miraculous
spring.

14

NO CROSBY, STILLS, AND NASH

Not young.
Just a couple of boomer travelers
on the train to Marrakech,
making local and express stops.
Second-class seats mostly occupied
by Moroccans speaking loud,
dusty Berber above the clacking
roar, dry landscape flashing by
the open windows.

A young gal in fashionista shades
and an Erykah Badu headdress
chews gum and undulates
to private soulful tunes
from ear buds in the aisle ahead.

Comes the call to prayer,
a transformation begins:

Down comes the hipster turban,
unraveling into a wide shawl.
Eyes closed, now devout, she
bows her newly covered head,
raises open hands
and prays solemnly seated in place.

A few moments later,
ritual complete,
she reassembles her ensemble,
grabs another stick of gum,
hooks up to her music,
and freshens up the make-up.
She flashes a pretty grin.
strikes a pose, and returns to
funkin the IRT to the Bronx.

15

3.EPIPHANIES OTHER RANDOM REALIZATIONS

gobsmacked in a night blizzard

The humless
electricity
of snow
falling
heavily
through
nights sky
charges
my synapses
with crackling
currents
surging me
buzzing
flushed
head-on
out
into

luminous
darkness.
Crunching
heavy booted
through
novocaine
surfaces
tilting
my head
to excited
facetingles
catching
lace webs
dissolving
on lashes
feverishly
butterfly kissing
the night's infinitely
dense
deluge

16

PRIVATE DANCER?

casually asked her to dance
mostly cause she was swaying
to the music as we spoke.

surprised how quickly we fell into
the same flow. could hardly believe
how easily we became synchronized
with each other's every move.

as if we had a special, almost
spiritual connection. as if I'd
met my other dancing half.

exhilarated. delighted.
even a touch besotted.
grooved through several numbers.
express soul train to infatuation.

after a bit took a break to pee.

rushed back to the sight of her

on the floor with my close buddy.
this guy, one of those hippy dippy
swirling dervish type dancers
the kind seen spinning on the edges
of Dead concerts: elbows out, arms
swimming in circles, body endlessly,
ecstatically, twirling.

I, by contrast, fancied myself
a gritty, funky, pivot shifting,
booty shaking, shoulder shrugging,
urban, R&B kinda guy.

the gal danced totally
in sync with my hacky-sacky pal.
they moved like shadows of each other.

hard swallow. deep sigh.

hung back. watched from the buffet
she paired with a few more guys.
each time she took just seconds
to figure out her new mate's moves
before transforming into his one and only
private dancer.

a pause to re-inflate. lick wounds.
smile wryly. remind myself once again...
the lesson of the ancient hunter:

the mirror is a dangerous
place to fall in love.

17

LOVE, FROST

Late that autumn
we walked
the Wissahickon
kicking through remains
of a brilliant summer and flashy fall.
wood smoke insinuated itself
between us. the forest looked
forlorn. embarrassed to be
so laid bare. It was over
but for a few bits
that refused to let go.
Random clinging leaves.
Roots tangled in the underneath.
The hard frost had just arrived.
No more Indian summers.
Our eyes tearing in the chill,
we trudged irresolutely. Resigned.
An ineluctable fall
from a sizzling season
to shivers and cold breaths.
Walking not touching

but still attached.
Finally we hugged
insulated by heavy layers
from our bodies'
reminiscences.
Then we tore apart
in separate directions
braced against
the approaching winter.

18

AWAKENING, AROUSING

He emerged abruptly
from the depths, back
creaking in harmony
with the ancient four poster.
Craned his neck to see the clock
confirm he had slept long and well.
Outside, rain gurgled through downspouts;
tires droned on the roadbed.
The room was dim
with drizzly morning light,
chilly damp beyond
the snug cocoon of blankets.
She was asleep next
to him facing away.
Soundless. Still. Fathoms beyond.
Turning to take her in,
he felt his already swollen self
ache tangled tight against
his pajama pants: swollen
restrained prisoner.
He reached down to free himself;

loosened and pushed down his bottoms;
yanked his top slow-motion over-and-up,
thrilling to
the chill of bare skin
against the cool sheets.
He inched toward her, ever so softly
touched his palms
against her flanneled bottom,
caressing her haunches slowly,
gradually beginning to knead,
climbing with inexorable purpose
up her back, thumbs creeping
and pressing along her spine,
then fingering a soft rhythm
at the base line of her neck.
She emerged in stages:
barely perceptible groans
eliding into tuneful moans,
morphing into sweet groggy
sighs. Then, when ready,
she slipped back her leg
to reach out her foot
to touch his toes with hers.
Delighted, he grabbed the hem
of her night gown; pulled up,
yanking past her hips as she raised
them just in time.
He slid himself up against her,
skins colliding in startle-body delight,
nerve endings sparking another
awakening celebration.

19

PROMPTED BY A
BILLBOARD

If you were here,
I'd be home by now
in the squint of your lips
and the giggle of your eyes
with your smile wrapping
round my face
and your hands
whispering soothing messages
on the back
of my unknotting neck.
If you were here,
I'd be sinking softly into
your cushions,
lounging languidly on
your soft recliner
and drinking toasts to our
comfortable
comforting life
surrounded by

your bric-a-brac,
your draperies,
your window treatments,
and the surprisingly
soothing embrace
of the colors
and textures
of every furnishing
brought to decorate our rooms.
If you were here.
I'd be in very soft
repose...
in the padded
corners and in the dark
crannies
and in the fuzzy
crevices
and on
the smooth
edges...
home...
by now...
already.
Please hurry back...

20

EPIPHANY

he had been around
the moon lit block
four times already.
each turn brought
the same results:

baby girl
would
settle down
into the Snugli
in the rhythm
of his stride
and soon nod off
for the quarter mile
of soft suspended
bouncing...

back ever-so
carefully through
the front door,
only for the child

to wail
uncontrollably
just as he tried
to place her back
into her crib.

last nerve frayed
deeply sleep
deprived.
primitively
needing
reprieve
or rescue
an instantaneous
flash of rage
obliterates
all rationality.

replaced
instantaneously
by an overwhelming
urge to throw his baby
against the wall.

the impulse
twists and curls
him down,
bends him forward
in a protective shell
to shield the child
against his own fierce fury

in sync with

with his own father's
rage at it's worst.
he feels that ire
from inside out.

he is not
like him.
he IS him.

viscerally
transported
behind
the fiery eyes
that scream
as loud
as any shout
he ever heard
his father
bellow.

and he is somehow
also still himself.
hyperaware
all at once
of the devastating danger
to this helpless being
in his arms
which are
fortuitously
frozen in fear,

he gently puts
the baby down

inside the bassinet
aware fully
and with absolute clarity
the dreadful truth.

I can not ever hit this child.
I must not ever hit this child.
I will not ever hit this child.

he calls upstairs
to his sleeping wife
in a voice
that bears
the gravity
of the moment:

"Please come help.
I'm afraid.
I can't do this.
any more tonight."

and she rose
and took the baby
asking no questions.

and the promise made
that night is kept

so that the child
be father to the man.

21

DANCING WITH MY DAUGHTER

tow head bobbing
dandelion bud.
joyfully curious.
inventive.
intentionally busy
inside the gentle
buzzing of her universe:
dolly tea parties,
stuffed animal jamborees...
always atuned, reacting
to the music around her.

barely able
to stand, she'd
grab onto random
chair legs, shake
her diapered
bottom, smiling
broadly, joyful butt

pumping to the
household beats.

tunes selected
expressly for
booty shakes.
we'd silly-dance
to "My House",
"Rocky Raccoon"
"Octopus's Garden",
and "Oh Superman!"

lifted her, soaring overhead
rushing room to room to
"Rocket Man", chem-trails
of giggles in our wake.

kid songs, rock and roll,
African beats, Indian
ragas. Celtic, New Age,
Folk, and RnB...
back-up
tracks for all the family's
comedies, tragedies and
farces. surround
sound. interwoven.
embedded in
each episode:
daily life.

at school, she
moved with beats
that bolstered

social securities.
liked what she knew.
knew what she liked.
tune horde to match
any's. curiosity
for new cool stuff.
a way to talk about
"the music".

shared discoveries
with dad who beamed
with pride, admired much.
added her grunge
and hip hop
to his playlists
and traded
up his new-found
trip hop samples.

she got her style together.
got her cool boots.
found her clique.
her voice.
her fashion,
her crushes...

of course, dad brought
her to her first arena
concert. blew her
preteen mind: Janet
prancing/dancing.
pyrotechnics.
the roaring mob.

of course, she booked
him to chauffeur
her posse to all their
first shows. of course,
she got him to chaperone
a pre-teen gaggle
(inside, but afar)
at all-age venues.

of course, she had
him drive a carful
of her buddies,
shepherd
and protect them
from the mosh pits
and surging crowds
at the Lalapalooza
extravaganza.

but he was
gobsmacked
by darling daughter's
ambush attack
smack dab
in the middle
of a George Clinton
funkathon.

sweet girl picked
her moment.
wandered through
the crowd. found

her father hanging
solo. near the back.
offered him a hug.
commenced
to dance with him
unselfconscious.
casual. a hipster
cool remix rendition
of a thousand
homemade
bootie shakes.

he was
a tad
astounded.

touched. and
unabashedly
proud
to somehow
be so blessed.

this gracious,
grateful interlude
became a ritual
(sometimes
surrounded
by a circle
of her besties)
each time he
served as
designated
driver.

till they would,
as must they should,
find their own ways
to concert venues.

but he would still
remember. fondly.

22

ASPARAGUS PEE

the smell of
asparagus pee
arrives gently:
wafting suddenly
from underneath,
a stealthy
pungent cloud
of vaguely familiar
surprise
momentarily
disorienting:
the odor on
wet grass
after minks
mate?
a pig's breath
after eating
truffles
cashews
and hay?
no. just

that funky
nut creamy
alfalfa
smoked
dry mist
arising from
the water
below.
and you
realize
you've
been here
before:
"oh,
that's
right,
I had
asparagus
for
dinner"

23

HOW TO LAY A TABLE OF COMFORT FOODS

Spread a beautiful
cloth on a long table:
nestle your browned-in-butter
till-almost-crunchy
pierogies with
plenty of sautéed onions
around your grill-seared
kielbasa on a crowded platter
next to a dish of
succulent loin of pork
with soft mounds
of creamy mashed
potatoes slathered
in gravy next to a
slow-cooked crumble-to-
the-fork rump roast
alongside a big
plate of hot tamales
and Chile Rellenos

swimming in salsa roja
on a bed of dirty rice.
Add a bowl of paprikash
chicken with dumplings
and a pot of sausage &
spicy meat balls and
saucy tagliatelle
next to a tureen of osso buco.
Then stack your loaves
of crusty French bread
in a large basket and
invite your lover.

24

THE ARCHAEOLOGY OF A GATHERING AESTHETIC:

a Villanelle

Our home, a shrine to a life of gathering.
A reliquary of mementos, fascinations, finds:
beautiful things from around the world.

An Arts and Crafts array in a Tudor dwelling:
ceiling beams and mahogany framing the display.
Our home, a shrine to a life of gathering

textile coverings for walls and floors:
fabrics, weavings, kilims, and rugs:
beautiful things from around the world.

On the mantel: pottery, carvings and stone;
totems and masks on the sills and stairs.
Our home, a shrine to a life of gathering.

A collection of delights and reminders
of traveling, hunting, and encountering
beautiful things from around the world.

The colors, the shapes, the textures and lines
define our taste and declare our style.
Our home, a shrine to a life of gathering
beautiful things from around the world.

25

THE MORNING AFTER
THE NIGHT BEFORER

sleep dirty
gritty eyed
up-all-night
desolate.

resolutely
gut torn
pissed at
the mood
yo-yo:

the harpies
buzz drone
a hum
of fading
recriminations:

replays without

do-overs.
mind high
and dry.
awash
in tidal
brain waves.

defiant,
resolute to not
go with
the bounce
this time.

he sways
to the dirge.
rides the groove
in the vinyl
all the way
to the crack
where the record
jerks back
a screechy
refrain.

a grudging
nudge
of the
needle
might
bump
that tune
forward
to ride

to where
the arm lifts
and the sad
song fades
into memory

but he stands
flat footed.
still replaying
the taunting
loop

26

IT'S ALWAYS NOW

now doesn't slip
until you grab

here is the middle
of a series of moments

when need not matter
if you are here now

life is most electric
in the midst of
an instant

27

MEDITATION

our universe
expands
and contracts
within and without
our losses.

we can ride
the reverberations
or resist

but either way
we are altered

loss is both
hollowing
and defining.

loss creates
form to shape
our very being

as we
reconstruct
our deconstruction
we recreate
ourselves.

or don't.

28

AFTERLIFE MEDITATION

closer to the end, open to dissolve

first

came

the letting go

from

doing

to being.

(still on-going.)

now the process

shifts

to becoming

still

(without squirming)

holding

gently

(without squeezing)

the horrible

holy

peaceful

transitioning

from being

to nothingness.

spend

a little time

most days

contemplating

and

inviting

peaceful

dissipation:

sit

becoming

void:

clearing

brain.

breathing.

empty out.

detaching

dissolving

diffusing

awareness:

atomization.

dispersal.

it

gradually

begins

to feel

just

as

possible

as

inevitable.

amen.

29

PRAYER

I wish to live
in the realm
of the senses.
dwell whenever
possible
within breath
and being,
experience
ongoing hunger
and
elegant
sufficiency,

then dissolve
into the elements
from which I came.

30

CODA

**Reaching a Milestone:
An Autobiographic Elegy/Eulogy to Years
of Intentional Wandering without a Compass.**

emerged from the hodgepodge
of north jersey in the fifties:
dove full of anxiety and insecurity into
a history of (western) ideas program,
got swept up in cascading torrents
of social protest and anti war
turbulence, theater of cruelty,
NEW YORK CITY,
drugsandsexandrockandroll,

a first big love,
St Mark's Place, The Thalia,
the Lower East Side,
the Berrigans,
the New Left,
The Voice,
Marat/Sade,

demonstrations,
draft counseling...

hitched a ride on my first love's wanderlust,
cadging a lift to a faraway land that blew
my parochial mind. scared me shitless.
rearranged my boundaries. and began
a series of lifelong intermittent safaris
to places, peoples, cultures, cuisines, crafts,
music, landscapes, and panoramas.

along the way
was awed, enthralled,
infatuated, broken hearted,
obsessed, engaged,
demoralized, detached
and re-invigorated
many times over.

lost and found my path
literally and figuratively.

inherited a buzzy dyslexic brain
given to moodiness
and having almost no sense
of direction, depended
on the kindness of strangers
and adventurous smart women
to help navigate my way through
a perilous but alluring world.

married two of these women, each
wonderful in different ways.

each a pathfinder.
both exceptional travelers.
each a Sacagawea.
one, my travel partner/guide
on a two-and-a-half-year sojourn
to Southern Africa: exotic, exhilarating,
challenging, and life changing.
she was a quietly brilliant woman with whom
parting was sweet, painful and inevitable sorrow.
leaving each of us better off and wiser.

the other, my navigator
over the very long haul
of discovery, joy, struggle,
conflict, and loving resolves.
my life partner/travel buddy/gardening
coach/co-parent/nana-to-my-papa/
hostess-to-my-most-whatever,

calm-to-my-storm.
my patient steady other.

had bumps,
reversals,
twists and turns.
re-found a rhythm.
and a deeper friendship
on the trek through
the extenuated adolescences
which seem obligatory
for some of us
who tear up their roots
to find other fields

in which to plant themselves.

on the way
discovered
the humbling,
extraordinary joy
of fatherhood.
an unexpected bond.

a daughter who miraculously
became a good friend.

then won the lottery
late in life:
a grandchild:
nothing quite like
nor even remotely close
in all the world:
 grand-baby love.

basically, life's been good.
better than I might have expected.

traveled in fascinating circles.
took wild tangents.
discovered my way back.
took some chances.
followed my heart and talents.
met some critically helpful mentors.
had some extraordinary luck.
made some deep and special friendships.
learned a craft.
embraced a career.

fashioned my own counseling style
found good hard work
in a field I actually enjoyed,
for a cause I could believe in,
and stumbled upon
passionate interests
to consume me
as I played
almost as hard as I worked.

taught secondary school in Zambia,
ran psych groups at the state mental hospital,
was an outpatient therapist in a mental health center,
did a stint as an assistant professor,
designed and managed an agency
domestic violence program,
ran a continuing education series,
organized a national DV conference,
trained therapists,
lectured grad students,
designed treatment programs,
ran my own DV clinic.
gave scores of professional talks,
appeared on local tv, radio and
a segment of 20/20.

heard thousands of personal stories,
was touched by the real-life dramas
of a myriad of clients,
was schooled by black culture,
informed by queer folk,

developed a daily exercise ritual

of rigorous morning walks to chill
my brain and reinforce my heart.

meandered across the US,
Mexico, Central America, East Africa
much of Europe and chunks of Morocco.
rode a camel in the Sahara;
camped overnight.

wandered the warrens of many old cities,
browsed and shopped. browsed and shopped.
bought a bit of hashish in several foreign countries

dove into countless
new and used record/CD bins,
took lots of sick days to toboggan
through scores of snow storms.

played with abandon and limited skills
both volleyball and touch football for decades.

with dogged dyslexic determination
became an episodically avid reader.

for sheer joy and a fascination
with narratives watched
many thousands of movies.

hunted and gathered
myriads of bargains
from Marshall's,
department store basements,
and whatever sale rack

in whatever shop
we/I wandered into
on our travels.

hiked trails,
played in mountain streams,
chased waterfalls,
tent camped and RV-ed
whenever possible.

dug a deep pond. filled
it with fish and frogs.
tended it for twenty-odd
years. built a five foot
waterfall with enough
meticulous artifice
to resemble actual nature.

became a decent beginner gardener.

evolved into a fervent cook,
an enthusiastic food shopper.

discovered, with little surprise,
I had become my mother
feeding random visitors
at the drop of a hat.

went to dance clubs
with small posses
of superannuated
raver-wannabes
in my late forties,

fifties and early sixties.
lived to tell some tales...

threw many big house parties:
for a wide range of ages, races, and
quite a variety of orientations.
danced for hours to playlists
I slaved over for weeks.
prepared elaborate buffets
for these soirées.

collected music
from around the world,
funk, soul, rock, folk, jazz,
hip hop, trip hop,
electronica, Dub, and reggae,
and a bit of classical.

attended scores of concerts.

wrote poetry,
made collages,
strung beads
posted a gazillion
things on Facebook,

happened upon
a sense of style,
enjoyed fashion,
fabric, line and look.
(my head bobs
in mom's direction)

discovered profound delight
in nest building with my wife,
festooning our place
with objects from round
the world.

feel lucky. and blessed.
with scars and wry grins
to prove it.

pull my white hair
back and over my thinning
pate to a tail that sways
on daily walks.

tie a topknot
before I shower.
notice a hint
of grandma Sophie
(from Bosnia and Hoboken)
in the bathroom mirror.
she, who made mad chicken
paprika and never really cared
much for my dad
who also haunts me nightly
while I brush my teeth.
the innuendo of his smirk
suggesting maybe he sees
quite a bit of similarity.

give or take a few extra cards
I got dealt to my hand just
because of when and where

I sat down to the table,

this could, indeed, be true.

also true is that
it is my intention
to glide very
much more slowly
to the end of this ride,
savoring my senses
even as they may diminish.

want very much also
to be more still.
to stop so much doing...
be...more...mindful...
be as present as possible
to family. to friends.
to myself and
to a sober awareness
that I and this
will all dissolve.
that the business
of doing must
gracefully release
into a stillness
of simply being

and into an acceptance
of everything as it is
and was and will be:

nothingness.

and not me.

perhaps one day,
hopefully a while
from now,
the tombstone,
urn, or cardboard box
might have a short inscription.

something like:

> Cherished his Family.
> Was Skeptically Optimistic.
> Loved Beautiful Things and Crafted Language
> Cared. Worked Hard. Played Passionately.
> Enjoyed Feeding People Good Food.
> Eventually Became Still.

SPECIAL THANKS

I am very grateful to two dear, old friends who generously offered their time and expertise in the proofreading and editing of my original manuscript. Anne Schneller and Steve Laruccia were initial readers. Their keen eyes and aesthetic judgments contributed significantly to the choices made finalizing this volume. They were each quick to respond, thorough, and thoughtful.

I am also especially thankful to Bill Van Buskirk, who was originally instrumental in encouraging me to finally begin to publish the work I'd been writing for decades. He definitely sits atop my "But for Whom..."pantheon of patrons and cheerleaders. A recognized talent in the Philadelphia poetry scene, Bill's generosity towards me and other writers has been truly nurturing.

Must also bow and tip my beret to my loving wife, Gloria Detweiler, who has patiently offered me the space, time, support and permission to pursue my writing.